Being Martha's Friend

Also by Meg Mooney
For the Dry Country: writing and drawings from the Centre
(with artist Sally Mumford)
The Gap

Meg Mooney
Being Martha's Friend

Acknowledgements

I would like to acknowledge the support I received to work on this collection from a publishing fellowship awarded by Varuna, The National Writers' House, in partnership with Picaro Press. I am very grateful to Deb Westbury, my mentor under this fellowship, for her great support, and astute and respectful comments on my poems.

I would like to thank my friends in Aboriginal communities who have taught me about their country, especially Martha, who is the inspiration for this collection. I would also like to thank the friends who have listened thoughtfully to many poems. You have made all the difference. Lastly, many thanks to Sally Mumford for her wonderful drawing on the cover of this book.

Some of the poems in this collection have been previously published in *Best Australian Poems 2012* (Black Inc); *In the Pink, poems from the Garden* (small dog press, 2012); *Adrift* (Northern Territory Writers' Centre, 2010); *Best Australian Poems 2009* (Black Inc); *Fishtails in the dust: writing from the Centre* (Ptilotus Press, 2009); *Landscapes*, Vol. 4, Issue 1, 'Peripatetica: The Poetics of Walking', Issue 2, 'Sustainabilia': The Poetics of Sustainability', and Vol. 5, Issue 1 (Edith Cowan University, 2010–13).

Being Martha's Friend
ISBN 978 1 74027 999 4
Copyright © text Meg Mooney 2015
Copyright © cover & internal images Sally Mumford 2015

First published 2015 by
Picaro Press – an imprint of
GINNINDERRA PRESS
PO Box 3461 Port Adelaide 5015 Australia
www.ginninderrapress.com.au

Contents

About Being Martha's Friend — 7
Looking for ngamunpurru — 9
A different history — 11
Willowra camp — 13
Birdwatching during the Intervention — 15
A long way across the plateau — 17
Warumpi Hill — 19
The bush foods trip — 20
Being Martha's friend — 22
Ilpili — 25
How do I write this poem? — 27
Brown quails — 28
Not quite burning the books — 30
Community history — 33
For the future — 35
Holding country — 37
Mostly loss — 39
My town — 41
A visit home — 43
The reading — 45
Too much sorry — 48
Driving back from the community — 50
Visiting the spring — 52
How does it happen? — 54
Listening to the radio during the Intervention — 55
A rama world — 57
Sorry Day in Alice Springs — 59
Not forgetting — 61
Sandplain afternoon — 63
Belonging — 64
Martha at her outstation — 66

About *Being Martha's Friend*

This collection focuses on my friendship with a Luritja woman, Martha or Tjulyata, and travels with her around the country near the remote Aboriginal community of Papunya, 230 kilometres west of Alice Springs, often in search of local plant and animal foods.

I first met Martha when I worked as a Literature Production Supervisor for the bilingual program at Papunya School twenty-seven years ago. Martha was the cleaner at the school. We were about the same age, mid-thirties. She was already a grandmother carrying around her grandchildren, as she would their children.

As a natural scientist, I was excited about moving to the desert but hadn't thought much about Aboriginal people. I hoped I'd get on OK with them. Now, Papunya is one of my homes. I only lived there for four years but have visited regularly, in the last fourteen years mainly through a program I run supporting two-way learning about the bush in remote community schools.

My knowledge and love of the central Australian bush, particularly its plants and animals, has grown in the decades I have spent here. This strong interest of mine I share with Martha, who grew up living off these plants and animals.

Martha and I don't have lots of words in common. I'm not fluent in Luritja and she doesn't speak a lot of English, but somehow we have become good friends.

Being Martha's Friend is about times, some wonderful, some hard, that I have spent with Martha and other people from central Australian Aboriginal communities, and related accounts from my life in the Centre.

Looking for ngamunpurru

Martha directs me along a dirt road
cutting straight from the airstrip
to the outstation near the foothills
the other tracks, pottering across the plain,
are no good now she says

we can't find the old way from the outstation
so we head along the main route
towards the bare range looking over us
its ridges and valleys mauve and dark blue

we haven't gone far when Martha shouts
to stop, go back – she's spotted a bush
among the spinifex and sennas
some distance from the road

we find it covered with white star-flowers
Martha's great-grandchildren point out a few berries
drops of green among the fine leaves
'not ready yet' smiles Martha
'that awalyurru same' – another shrub with berries
we see some the next day, she's right of course

so we go back east to her outstation, away from that time
when the old ladies hit branches with sticks
to make the berries fall on a cloth
used a long wooden bowl to winnow out the leaves
soon the dish was full of shiny, dark fruit
Martha picked by hand, her beautiful face
concentrating as she filled a large milk can
from the little stand of bushes in the foothills

I wore a favourite yellow and black skirt
took photos, not knowing the old ladies
would collect ngamunpurru like this only a few more years
the younger, less-skilled women would not be so keen
tracks would close up, weeds threaten
and this bounty would end

Author's note: Martha is the whitefella name of my friend Tjulyata. For no particular reason, in some poems I have called her Martha and in others Tjulyata.

A different history

We lose the old track in places
loop around bloodwood trees, witchetty bush
till we find the faint tyre marks again
finally go over a high dune to the lake
that has appeared like a lost story
a great silvery sheet stretched between red dunes
where usually there's just rusty soil, mulga, coolabah trees

as we stand looking at all that water
the strangeness of flotillas of ducks
awkward shapes of egrets in gum trees
my friend points out an old windmill
tells me that when his people came –
or were taken – to the big community
there was too much fighting
so the old people brought their families
and all the young men here, back near their country

recently I found a booklet by another friend –
she's passed away now, too young –
in the story, she's a child riding horses and camels
collecting bush tomatoes with her friends
knocking down budgies (to eat) with pieces of barbed wire
then her family moves here, to Lampara
'Lampara was a good place' she wrote

I don't want to leave the clean crimson shore
spreads of coolabah shade
but we head off along the lake
watch it disappear behind us

catch another old track, more of a gully now
the troopies crawl around thickets of wattles
the schoolkids scream when they see kalinykalinypa
break off the big yellow spikes, suck the honey from them
and the little red bell-flowers of ngarrankura

everyone is happy car-walking along this track
it feels like we've slipped back with the old people
roaming familiar country, feasting in these good times
I can almost hear them laughing

Willowra camp

My teacher friend Maisie
sings softly to me
songs she's made up
about animals, syllables, numbers
we're watching the old women
draw graceful strokes
of red and white ochre
on each others' breasts
chanting, chanting
through the hot afternoon

the Nampitjinpas' swags are close by
wildly coloured blankets snuggled side by side
behind a straggly line of bushes
a few extra branches woven through
to protect the women and children
from the cold south-easterlies

the Napaltjarris' bedding over there
heads also to the south-east
the Nakamarras near the river

a rough camp to an outsider
but right and comfortable to those here
rows of swags in skin and family groups
guarded by windbreaks and little fires
open to the low scrub of the sandplain
for miles in every direction

the whitefellas on the southern, windy side
swags huddled among bushes
mine across the track, at a quiet distance

I open my eyes each morning
to a flood of red along the horizon
we travel around the great 'empty' plains
dig up yala, bush potatoes
gather round our campfires
to cook and talk into the night

when I go home
it seems very strange
to be shut up in a house

Birdwatching during the Intervention

As soon as we stop we hear them
'didyougetdrunk? didyougetdrunk? didyougetdrunk?'

a gentle waterfall of sound
sometimes close and insistent
mostly a little way off.

As I lie on red sand
criss-crossed with insect, bird, mice, lizard tracks,
whole new stories I can't read every morning,

it's little showers of orange-beaked finches that visit.
'Nyii-nyi, nyii-nyi, nyii-nyi'
they chatter urgently in Pitjantjatjara.

I walk along the vermilion dune
a lone human footprint
around tangles of white flowers.

Honeyeaters fly quietly
between scraggy trees
babblers complain loudly in gullies

till I head off across the plain
harsh and glittery in the afternoon
with thousands of little shiny stones

dark and mysterious in the long lake of shadow
as I return from the second dune at dusk –
quails rocketing off at my feet –

and we finally see,
like this is the old days
when whitefellas were few,

one car go past
on the track along the swale
where we're camped.

By the time we leave
I learn it's in the shoulders of the dunes, the sound,
in the dead bushes from the big fire a few years ago.

The large, brown shapes of wedgebills
their cheeky crests
disappear as I get closer

like they're telling me
you can't just look
and expect to see
in this country.

A long way across the plateau

there are hands, all sizes
red ochre on leached shelter walls
still clear after thousands of years

somehow my mind eases
among all these spread hands
in overhangs facing the warm north
between tall rock domes

we could be in an old paved town
carved out of sandstone
on the edge of a high cliff
pavements cracked into polygons
like the dolerite of Roman roads

we find the water
held by a curve of wall on a low flat –
a lone black duck screeches off –
and camp in this basin

the full moon rises perfectly
in the gap where the creek
drops into a canyon
the calls of the returning duck
comfort the night

my sorrow feels safe here
with so many other stories
among the passageways and caves

maybe this was a good place
where people took refuge for a while
ate rock wallabies, bush plums, figs

and after so many years of quiet
their spirits seem to welcome
sounds of laughter and talking into the night

Warumpi Hill

When I go to see Tjulyata
her carved face framed with long white hair
(I'm shocked when I hear people
call me ulkuwuman, old woman)
she asks me to give Nangala a lift to Three-Mile

I head off the wrong way, Nangala directs me back
we drive east, past mulga plains
thick with grasses, the pale yellow of autumn

suddenly I'm driving into that time
when I'd have billy tea with friends at sunset
this wide road just a track then

now the hills appear to our right
the small rise, the head
the bigger one, the thorax
behind that the largest ridge
lined up across the plain

I love that great honeyant
its fat boulders, rock plates with swirls of minerals
the track between the head and thorax
where you can see the full moon rising
the special slits with water on the ant's sides
its white staffs of gums, bright-leaved wattles

Nangala and I don't talk
just sit companionably
looking at this country
we've had the luck to have
to grow old in

The bush foods trip

Martha takes us to a river bank to look for katjutarri
they used to get lots there after rain, she says
now she finds the creepers from one plant
among clumps of buffel grass weed

old Tilau dutifully plonks down with a crowbar
digs up a couple of finger-sized pencil yams
but they're too old to eat
maybe the ladies were just humouring me
maybe they didn't want to say
katjutarri is gone from here now

anyway, everyone is relieved
to head for the sandplain to get akatjirri
we drive past a sea of spinifex
to country burnt a year ago
'Who burnt it?' I ask
'Someone. From that Yuendumu road'

the old ladies and schoolkids
are soon bending over little bushes
scattered on the red sand
the kids roll up their T-shirts
to make pouches for the yellow fruit
like pale, tart raisins
everyone loves akatjirri

some kids appear with green-skinned ipalu –
badly named 'bush bananas'–
the length of a child's hand
like unripe corn on the inside
when they're young and good to eat

they're popular, but not like akatjirri
it's tasty, fills you up
and there's so much of it
maybe it's more important
for the spirit of the country
to eat what's good and easy to get
than learn about the old plants

now the kids produce handfuls of skinny bush beans
the pods are yellow, full of fluffy seeds
not as common as ipalu
the old ladies can't think of its name
finally remember, 'pulpalangi! pulpalangi!'

Tilau bends over wangunu, a fine grass
Daisy and Elsie show me ankle-high yaalkara
their mothers used to make damper
from these grass seeds, they say, smiling –
it's hard to think of now, everyone uses white flour

I spread out samples of our finds
the ladies talk about them
an Aboriginal teacher videos the kids
practising the names they don't know
everyone is happy anyway
with our booty from the sandplains
still rich after fire and rain

Being Martha's friend

It's like this
I'm just starting to write
about how you grabbed my hand
yesterday, held it close between us
told those teachers
who've only been here a few years
'she's my friend, this one, from long time'
and we laughed

that was just after I'd said
no, I couldn't bring you back to town
it'd be night by the time we got there
I'd be too tired to have you stay
so you could pick up your great-granddaughter
take her home for the weekend –
and who was going to do that?

back at my desk, the phone rings
it's you, telling me your granddaughter
is at that camp in town
'you might take her a hundred dollars –
what time?' you ask
'three?' I suggest – that gives me a few hours

to follow you in my mind
around the burnt country
black twigs of shrubs, sooty grass, clear red sand
really good for seeing goanna tracks
each old lady has a following of kids
they disappear into the distance

I'm with you and two great-granddaughters
plus some schoolkids, related somehow
you read out the ground
a quick look at a hole with fresh diggings –
'that goanna gone, this way'
you follow winding furrows
of body marks, claw prints
with your old eyes
we strain to see

it's hot, no one is carrying water
you tap with your crowbar
listen to the ground
finally announce 'this one home'
plonk yourself down, start digging
'husband and wife here' you say
after a few minutes, you reach down
pull out a lithe yellow body
your hand firmly around its mouth
the kids scream, you hold it up for a photo
then whack its head on the ground
stretch down to get the other one

in two hours, three women get eight goannas –
the other woman, rama rama, a bit mad
sits on her own with none –
fires are lit to char the skin of the catch
then bury them in hot ashes
soon we're eating the fragrant white meat
of the husband and wife
the wife's round lollipop eggs

the women sit on the warm ground
eat quickly, gulp sweet billy tea
because the teacher says we have to go
so the kids can get back for school lunch
the women roll their eyes, grumble
climb into a troopie with their crowbars
sad to leave this country despite the midday heat

as I drop you off you ask
if I can bring your great-granddaughter
out to the community this weekend
'no, I can't' I say 'I'm too busy' –
and overwhelmed enough
with the drive before me
later this afternoon

and now I write this poem
this is how it is

Ilpili

I've driven for many hours, am exhausted
but as troopie-loads of kids and adults
settle under gidgee trees in a parkland of white grass
a part of me I'd half-forgotten wakes up

the kids swarm around three local rangers
one, the springs' traditional owner, is grey at forty
I knew his older brother, long dead
the younger brother shot himself accidentally at twelve –
I can still hear the wails roar through the community

we set marsupial mice traps on the plain
I remember how good it feels
to see the horizon in every direction
the youngest ranger is like his mother
easy with people
as chatty as a cooking show host

digging reptile traps on a red sand dune at sunset
I ask the third ranger about his father
still alive in his seventies –
I remember he got lost on a hunting trip once
drove around and around – afterwards, laughing,
drew a looping map of his travels

at dawn troopies full of bouncing kids
trundle off to check traps
one boy, a handful in the classroom,
sings loudly, looks out the window
grinning at his country

later the rangers take us to the springs
it's not long since there was drinking water here
deep pools in paperbark forest
now the water is putrid with camel dung, two trees are left
the rangers have mustered a hundred camels
set up a trough nearby to try and divert the rest

in the long afternoon, gangs of kids roam between gidgee camps
family and friendship groups across four schools kick footballs
sit and talk in the shade, climb trees for bush coconuts

at night the rangers show photos from cameras at the springs
the kids are happy to watch endless shots of camels drinking in the dark
dingoes, roos and eagles left only the day

that evening an elderly volunteer reading tutor
talks to me about his difficulties with communities here –
the litter, different work ethic and so on

I look out at the flickering orange hearts of gidgee fires
realise none of that matters to me now
'it feels like home to me' I say

How do I write this poem?

Maybe as a confession
I've been angry 15 times
I've been cranky 20 times
and often grumpy with friends

when they ask me to drop off some money –
they have no car, or even if they do
I need to go and get the cash
it's only every few weeks
when they're in town

it's not the money so much –
although that's got something to do with it –
but finding the time, or going out
when I wanted to stay at home

why can't I just say
'I'm sorry I can't do it
until this afternoon, tonight, tomorrow?' –
because they're probably hungry
they need to buy fuel, something

I've been shoe-horned into another reality
where you get money day-to-day
everyone has family
they have to share with
you can't hole yourself up
in a house on your own

Brown quails

I first see them scuffling around
between the lettuce and broccoli

plump little birds
black and brown hieroglyphs
on their bellies
mosaics with moving lines of silver
along their backs

they pass quickly around the vegies
briefly risk the open
four, six, maybe ten
now they're in the saltbush
I can see it wiggling
occasionally a head appears
with a bright red berry
stuck on the end of its beak

soon they're at the edge of the garden
do a wobbly run
down the no man's land of an open slope
through the long grass of the drain
necks stretched up the other side
and they're in the bush

they make this daring trek again
the quails, maybe often
a few times I see them, around dawn or dusk
their dark shapes catch my eye
or I notice saltbush or grasses stir
as if the plants are moving of their own accord
excited by the new or passing day

as I open or close the curtains
and glimpse these busy, haute couture chooks
rare visitors of big flood years
I think, *Why wouldn't I delight in this day?*
and the caterpillar range flushes deep pink

Not quite burning the books

1.

Cream metal louvres
stained with red dust
they don't keep out,
dirty lino tiles sloshed each afternoon
from a muddy bucket.
I spent years in this room,

with the clatter of folding, binding and stapling machines
mixed with fragments of gospel songs from a dying tape player,
continually rewound by young artists and transcribers
talking in long runs of words I couldn't understand.

The only texts in this language,
apart from some dictionaries,
the bible, a hymn book or two,
are booklets made in this room.

Stories about a young man running from a plane
thinking it was a devil in the sky,
revenge parties tracking down men
who'd stolen young women,
couples who married wrong way,
sometimes whole families
in feuds that went on for generations,
'all the Tjampitjinpa men' chained together
and taken off for killing cattle.

Readers with sentences like
Wati ananyi ngurrakutu
The man is going home
with a drawing of a man
walking toward a corrugated iron humpy.

Legends about warriors spearing giant, man-eating goannas,
a man full of spears who turns into a centipede,
western desert versions of Grimm's tales –
in one, dingoes devour a lost boy
after weeing on the log he's hiding in, to make it fall apart,
in another mountain monsters steal babies and roast them on fires.

All the hunting stories,
looking, looking, looking
and often finding
goanna, emu, kangaroo, bush turkey.
Tales of country full of food,
grubs, honeyants, berries, yams.

2.

The preschool has taken over the old printery,
no one knows where the books are.
I imagine piles of them –
stories the old people carried,
pictures the young artists drew,
sitting for hours at an old wooden table
etched with their names,
photos of an echidna cooking in coals,
an old woman grinding grass seed on a stone to make damper –
all these thrown next to old washing machines,
mattress skeletons and dead cars at the rubbish dump.

The acting principal hasn't seen the books,
thinks they got packed up at the beginning of the year.
All the white teachers are new since then,
later we find some of the Aboriginal aides knew.

There's only one room we haven't searched,
in a corner of the old printery.
None of the teachers have a key for the padlock
but the janitor does.
The little room is piled high
with boxes, filing cabinets, crates,
all the stories,
locked away
in the darkroom
to make sure English is taught better.

Community history

Kapunani does a timeline with the kids
first they stick the photo of an old humpy
on to butcher's paper –
vertical forked branches
support leafy ones
that curve down on each side –
she tells the children to write 1950

(in sorry camps, where people live
after a close relative dies,
you still see humpies made of branches
with canvas, sheet-of-iron, dirt floors
much easier to clean than a house)

next there is a picture of brick pillars
some walls left of a tiny house
like a gate house of a mansion
Kapunani writes, in language,
that people worked and 'sat down'
in these houses – 1969

the house after that is a bit bigger
she tells one of the children
his great grandmother lived there – 1970

the following photo might surprise some people
it's a humpy, the same shape as the other one
but made of corrugated iron
1980 is written against this

I can't resist saying
maybe she should show
some people lived in houses then too
so under the photo of the iron humpy
it says other people still lived in houses, 1982

then they move on to 2000
a large house with verandas
now people live in these, she writes
but we all know there aren't enough of them
and that isn't the whole story

For the future

Old Lena makes me
recite the litany
arrethe here see
athenge over there
atnyeme, *untyeye*
her country of medicines

her ailing mind
calls out to the plants –
still here
after all the changes

while the local rangers
video *aherre-intenhe* –
'kangaroo shelter' –
the old ladies gather
its glistening bunches of leaves

this is when you collect it
my friend says
when the flowers have dropped
all the sap is coming out

we talk about bringing the schoolkids here
to mash the leaves on grinding stones
as their great-grandmothers did
before people knew this life was ending

these days they boil the leaves in billies
sometimes my friend worries
this drink, and the ointments
made with blenders and oil,
might be too strong, used too often

but now she says to one of the rangers
'you might find out more about these medicines
how to make them work better than we did'

maybe she can see herself
in this young woman
eagerly taking in knowledge
not because she has to –
the way my friend did
travelling with her family –
but because while the minds of Lena
and a few others continue to hold
she still can

Holding country

1.

My friend says she wants to capture
all the plants, from when the rains
kept coming and coming
like they were meant to

endless greens of woolly cloak ferns, herbs in mulga woods
plains rippling with purple-white kerosene grass
creeks lined with sedges, and sundews
stuck with lemon butterflies

so my friend takes photos –
while long memories of open red plains
bronze rocks against blue sky
clean white sandy creekbeds
start to disappear, slip from my mind
and I wonder whether I should
try to hang on to them too

2.

At night in this new world of lush woods
I read a poem to my friend about the silences of frogs –
red-crowned toadlets, Wallum froglets, green-thighed frogs
their voices slowly fading from people's minds

I almost have to shout
over the calls of frogs
in the creek near us
we laugh – but then it's like the local frogs
have somehow mixed in memories
of their east coast relatives
there's an edge of sadness to their calling

later we track the whining double notes
of the little brown tree frog
and the loud see-saw *honk-honk, honk-honk*
of its larger green cousin
the frogs squat, their throats swelling,
in small echo chambers
under rocks in the trickling creek
now they surround us with their sound
like it could never be forgotten

After *The Silence of the Frogs*, Martin Langford

Mostly loss

1.

The whining double notes
of brown tree frogs
urh-uurrh, urh-uurrh
echo through my house
like the wet ground itself is calling
has soaked up the rain and come alive –

in a way it has, I hear the *bok, bok, bok*
of Spencer's burrowing frogs burst out
of drought-proof cocoons underground
and the long *baaaah, baaaah*
of another burrower, the sheep frog

I tick the three frogs off
happily in my mind
all present and correct

it's comforting to sleep
to this symphony of frogs
the same one that has played
for hundreds of years

2.

Then I remember a crippled old woman
telling schoolkids recently how as a child
she'd eaten almost all the animals
on the endangered species poster –

princess parrots, bilbies, possums,
great desert skinks, small rat-sized mulgara,
little wallabies, even tiny moles –
and me saying these animals are nearly gone
because of foxes, cats, competition from rabbits, stock

the old woman looked at me
like I was mad –
the animals' spirits are still in the ground
it's just that no one is doing their ceremonies

now I think of her people
dying too often, too soon
wonder if there are
any ceremonies for that

My town

It was that time when I felt
like I was in a car smash
for weeks, although it was really my son
who had crashed

I've just had my legs waxed
walk out on to the main street
when someone calls out, an Aboriginal bloke –
only whitefellas like quiet streets
it sounds like my name, which is short –
shouts often confuse me like this

I walk on, the calls continue
maybe it is my name
it could be Tjakamarra
I gave him some money a few days ago
I'll just ignore it

then a child yells my name, clear and high
down the street, I turn
see the boy and young couple
my teacher friends from the community
waving from the lawn –

if I didn't know them, I might think
this man and woman were drunks sitting there
wanting to sell cheap paintings
it's easy to get things very wrong in this town –

I'm not up to much chat but that's OK
they just want to say hello
and merry christmas

I walk back down the street thinking
they don't know but it's like they do
and having my name shouted down the street
helped somehow, like they were letting everyone know
to catch me, because inside I was falling

A visit home

I've never camped just here before,
although someone has, years ago –
there's some sheet of iron for a windbreak,
a scatter of rusty bully beef and milk cans.
But I know I'm home, can't take my eyes off
the purple ridge to the south,
the outline of rock I carry in my mind.

I love the black nights,
lying in my swag, feeling the distant beat
of rock bands in a nissen hut,
waking on soft red ground,

and sitting next to Tjulyata cooking kangaroo tails
on a scrap of fire outside her house.
We talk in a scattering of phrases
about the footy oval getting moved,
them not living at the outstation since the deaths,
my son, almost grown-up now,
the rain flooding the graveyard
where her sons are.

Her latest great-grandchild toddles past, Tjulyata tells me
he's called Duncan, after her younger son.
I'm shocked, 15 years ago her son's face
would have been blocked out
with black texta in school albums,
his name rarely spoken, and then in a whisper.
Is just Tjulyata's family doing this, or everyone?
Did I expect this culture never to change?

Tjulyata asks her daughter, the remaining child,
to give me photos of the two young men.
She wants me to blow them up,
to put on the dingy walls of her house.
How big? Her daughter points
to the air conditioner, they nod, like that.

Is it all the deaths?
The reason for this change?
Anyway, I'm glad Tjulyata
can look at pictures of her sons
say the names she loves.

The reading

A lively young girl appears
as we set out platters of food
on the veranda of the old church hall
on a balmy summer's evening

I give her a party pie
she says her grandma wants some food too
I say you have to read something to get food
we'll give her grandma the leftovers

the old lady and a few other women
sit on the lawns
a few canvases spread before them

people arrive for the reading
we move the platters
down on to the lawn
among our audience

I tell a friend I feel bad
about not giving the grandma some food now
she and the other ladies are probably hungry

my friend says they might not be hungry
and there are some drunks there
but I see her soon after
bundling up pies and sausage rolls
to take over to the women

the readings start, 'a creative response
to the Federal Government's intervention
in Aboriginal communities'
after a damning report on sexual abuse

one of the women selling paintings
gets up, glares at us, limps
with her canvas away from the noise

we have an Aboriginal reader to start
she talks about the intervention's disruptions
to family life in the community where she lives

the next woman recounts her decision
not to drive past Aboriginal people lying on the road
and her first encounter with one

I read my birdwatching poem
with allusions to the intervention
wish I'd read something with more feeling

a drunk woman
staggers towards the microphone
is led away

an angry white woman gets up
goes on about blame, on both sides
I can't listen to her

one of our group is giving
the drunk woman a parcel of food
later I see a white woman
laughing with this woman, walking off with her
and wonder at this friendship

some tourists have stopped
stand and stare at the speakers

another woman gets up
reads an endless letter to the prime minister
outlining failures of the intervention
which all of us here already know

I feel more and more ridiculous
in this tableau of mainly white women
declaiming from a lighted mound of lawn
under a gum tree
to a mainly white audience

surrounded by Aboriginal people
not listening but watching

it's not all bad
one speaker says sexual abuse
is an issue for all women
reads a moving poem about an abused girl

the Aboriginal woman ends with her poem about town camps
'you call it a filthy town camp, I call it home'

after the reading, I walk along the mall
with the almost empty platter
people yell out for food
I yell back that there's only sauce left

Too much sorry

1.

Orange ground raked bare
a woman sits near a sheet-of-iron shelter
black beanie over hair hacked short

you hold out your right hand
I sit down, grasp your rough palm
as I should, but keep hold of it

you sob, tell me bits of the story in clear English –
not the usual mix with local phrases
neither of us fluent in the other's language
we haven't needed a lot of words to be friends

your granddaughter, the little girl's mother,
is coming back today
on that same road
not hurt – in body at least

you look up, move my leg gently
away from sand-covered coals
I'd clumsily plonked down beside

I ask about the two girls
who've just lost their father and little sister
you point under the low curve of iron
one sister raises her beanied head
holds out her hand to me
burrows back into an auntie's lap

as you sit in your dusty black T-shirt and skirt
doing what needs to be done
looking after the children, as always
I sit close to you from a world away
you stroke my soft thumb

2.

We've known each other since we were young women
me wearing colourful skirts, you bright bandanas
I'd finally moved to the desert
you were already a grandmother

in the two and a half decades since,
you've lost your beloved younger son
your son-in-law, and your other son
who was retarded, like my brother

now we talk about your old husband, not buried yet –
that death was before all this
I ask what you need, you point at blankets, tea, roo tails, flour
say you want clothes, someone threw your bag in the fire
then you ask for brown sugar *just a small one*
and lemon drink *that sweet one*

it doesn't seem right to let go
of your hand, but I do
go off, all the time thinking of you
sitting in the dirt with your head bent

Driving back from the community

My friend is yelling
on the rough road I struggle to catch
his fragments of English
it's about all the fighting in town
Whisky's wife dying in hospital
people getting blamed, attacked
some other story, from another community

the land is criss-crossed
with lines of tragedy
and in the town at the centre
they explode

suddenly my friend waves downwards
I slow, there's a corner coming up
then I realise it's not that

just off the track
a rectangle of red ground
is marked out with star pickets
linked by a chain
and fairy lights

inside the rectangle
bunches of pale pink roses
blue iris, white daisies
in concrete containers
a cross

not far away
a plain cross and flowers
for the little girl's father
who drove too fast around that corner

I saw the child's mother yesterday
a solemn young woman now
looking after the two older children
and her grandmother
while her mother lives in a faraway city
painting and drinking

I put my plastic carnations
on a cow-chewed bush
inside the rectangle
my old friend and I
pull a broken bit of chain
back on to a star picket
tidy up the lights and their solar cells
we stand for a moment
he says a prayer to 'Our Father'

'It was good to see that,' he says
as we walk away
'I'm glad I saw it'

Visiting the spring

It's us four whitefellas in the end
one of the young rangers would like to come
but the others think we're mad
huddle around the fire as we head off

the rangy land council bloke
drives wildly across stony foothills
squeezes the troopie between witchetty bushes

then we stop, turn on our torches
a wall of quartzite rises before us
high into starry sky

we walk beside this cliff
past red grevillea lanterns
yellow balls of curry wattle
we know cover these foothills by day

beetles and backswimmers
cruise in the creek
frogs swim stretched-out for the shadows
pale rock is as smooth as temple steps

we pull ourselves up them
into a narrow gash
see a single large frog
a keeper of these permanent pools

higher up we sit around a pond
like holy water
held by vertical walls
studded with smaller frogs

before we leave, another keeper
slides towards us
the biologist picks up the python
fat from feasting on mice and frogs

on the way back to camp
there's a new feeling between us
like we've found
something we were missing

the rangers, having a quiet smoke
around the fire, are relieved to see us
don't say we shouldn't have gone there at night
maybe they understand that us whitefellas
need to look everywhere for what we've lost

How does it happen?

Does it start with the drive along the range, tall shaded cliffs, crimson velvet?
Or when we turn off, the ute swims through buffel grass,
one set of tyre tracks our guide?
Or is it finally getting to the creek, its smooth spread of white sand?

Maybe it's the easy way you break logs,
put them in a dip you make in the sand,
I collect kindling, light the fire,
you remembering how your grandfather did this
when your family walked these creeks with camels, in times now lost,
me thinking of picnics with my parents and siblings
in far-off hills long ago.

Now we sit on the sand in the sun,
a view down the creek of steep, purple slopes.
You talk of your people meeting to discuss problems, make plans,
how hard it is when nothing happens.
I listen, pour tea from a billy, stir in powdered milk –
you took some to your brother in jail, he doesn't like Longlife milk.

When we leave I'm not tired anymore, you seem lighter,
it's like the spirit of your country is in us,
as you say: 'that's how we think about things, my people.'

Listening to the radio during the Intervention

We gather round the old radio
under the nursery shelter:
the nursery manager
the young green corps mob
doing mulberry cuttings
Audrey sitting on a stool in the sun
me and another project worker.

We sit on concrete blocks, milk crates,
the donga steps, an old metal bench,
listen to our boss on a local radio station.

He's talking about the government axeing CDEP
the work-for-the-dole scheme
that most of us are paid by.

The government is replacing CDEP
with back-to-work training and counselling.
Our boss runs a program like that too,
we all know how hard it is for most people
to get to that training
let alone a proper job

because they're sick, their family's sick
someone just died, a stabbing, a car accident
no one to leave the little kids with
no sleep because of the drunks
all reasonable excuses.

I look at Audrey
a tiny middle-aged woman
who can do a mean limbo.
In the last decade
between drinking parties and fights
trips to her family's outstation
she's had work she liked
potted up thousands of plants.

Our boss is getting angrier
he says the government mob lied to him.
I'm surprised by his vehemence –
he'd guessed CDEP was on the line.

Around the radio,
we laugh uneasily.

A rama world

Tjulyata is sitting on the ground
sweeping glass and dirt
with a brush into a little pile
she gives me her weary smile
'petrol sniffers last night, rama' she says

her daughter is still in town painting
Tjulyata doesn't like it in town
'ramalingku!' too much humbug
her little puppy jumps on her now, she picks it up
'rama rama this one' she laughs – just a bit mad

I ask her about murrtja
fat-tailed marsupial rats
say Narlie took us near Warumpi Hill –
lots of katakali (lily root to make your hair grow)
but only tracks of tjunginpa (mice) –
'does Narlie know murrtja?' I ask
'yes, she knows' says Tjulyata
'rama that one'

Tjulyata, of course, has seen
the tiny tracks of murrtja
on a road out of town
as she's going past in a car

on the way there we talk
about the policeman who's cheeky –
that means nasty –
and the administrator, he's rama too
has kicked out the storekeeper –
'he was a good man, that old man' –
so he can take over the shop

Tjulyata and I walk around spinifex
find lots of murrtja tracks
in the morning the schoolboys run to collect
the traps my co-worker and I set –
only three sandy mice –
but the boys won't walk with Tjulyata
to learn about murrtja tracks
'rama rama' she says
their teacher yells at them
they ignore him
'lazy one, that man' she says, 'rama'

Sorry Day in Alice Springs

I miss most of the words
because I forget it's on
but the few I hear
make me cry at once

because they're saying
the wrong that everyone sees
in the streets of our town
is a big problem for this country

because we're faced daily
with the trouble and sickness
that's come from that wrong
and most of us, including me
turn away from it
most of the time

because this wrong
affects all of us in this town
and it feels like
the rest of the country
has no idea

and we can't talk to them about it
because they'll never understand
from their all-white suburbs
or just get more racist

because the words talk
of people coming together
and you don't often see
a white person
walking with a black person
in this town

because it sounded like
he really meant it
and people believed him

Not forgetting

There are shoals of daisies
in the mulga woods
like someone has wandered around
splashing pale pink paint on the ground
far into the distance
mirror-in-mirror magic

out of a bottle opened rarely
by the right winter rain
comes this dusty sweet smell
fine rose-paper petals

I last saw woods flooded
with this fairy floss light
almost half a lifetime ago
when I'd finally moved to the desert

now I follow the islands of pink
away from the track
find big clumps of spinifex
died off in the centre, grown outwards
to form wide yellow rings on the red sand

they're like a gathering of sculptures
in memory of when
people walked this country
burning here and there
so some old spinifex was saved
for the animals that needed it

locals still hunt goanna nearby
but on the edge of the mulga
I come across an old camp, long undisturbed
a few dozen rusty cans, tobacco tins
a handful of little odd-shaped bottles
poke out of the ground –

containers for ointments or tonics
from the time of the ration station
half a century or so ago
when people first came in from the bush

I wonder what they were thinking
did they know how much was lost?

carpets of flowers like this
might not come to these woods again –
buffel grass weed uses fire
to eat its way through mulga

I take the bottles, clean them
line them up on the windowsill in the sun
a row of uncertain messages from the past

but somehow a sign of hope
of something continuing
for now at least

like the pink paper daisies

Sandplain afternoon

I'm walking with my friend Tjulyata
Kapunani and Isabel
we're supposed to be looking for tracks of murrtja
a little, endangered marsupial
but even I know we won't find them
in this burnt country

Tjulyata's great-grandchild picks akatjirri –
tart yellow raisins
chases little lizards
between grass clumps and fan flower bushes
fireweeds in the red sand

the sun is beginning to go down
there's no hurry, nothing we have to do
might be find goanna
pick akatjirri

it's hot but somehow the heat suits me
I don't want to rush back
to a waterhole with friends
like in my younger days here

always at home on this great sandplain
now I find the rhythm of these women
hunting easily
resonates in me too

we look at tracks
plants growing back after fire
I carry the little girl
follow Tjulyata

Belonging

Just like I will never be
an eighteenth century naturalist,
see the southern coast
before it was 'settled',
or bandicoots scamper
along the banks of the brown river
I grew up beside,
that river before it was brown,
tangles of lignum growing in its swamps,

I will never be indigenous.
It is not my lot
to belong to a landscape,
for it to own me,
to wave my hands and say
'my dreaming that one, always there'.

My land is that place with patchworks of green,
handwoven hedges, lime woods –
going there was like climbing into a picture
from my childhood story books,
complete with foxgloves and primroses,

but I soon found myself searching
for less tamed landscapes,
places with less people,
eventually came back to this home
of my grandparents' grandparents
but not their grandparents.

Still, I wonder if I will ever say
without hesitation,
like those old people in the desert,
'this is my country!'

Martha at her outstation

I drive south from the community
towards the purple mountains
turn off along a dirt track
am followed by a line of electricity poles
to a cluster of tin sheds and houses
surrounded by old mattresses, tyres, bits of machinery

Martha comes out of a small, concrete house
she's tall, with the skinny legs and slim figure
of a woman who's always walked a lot –
hunting goannas, collecting grubs, honeyants, berries,
walking to the shop, the clinic, the council office

her short hair is grey now, like mine
but she's still beautiful
sits down on an upturned flour tin
in a sunny corner of her veranda
gestures to the tin beside her, smiles

I sit down, say I'm sorry
I didn't bring any secondhand (clothes)
give her some money
she tells me her grandson has two children now
that was his wife I just saw
Martha's English is limited
I don't like to make her speak it much
feel shamed by my Luritja

so we sit in the sun
two women from different worlds
who've known each other for over two decades
since she was the cleaner at the school where I worked
I don't see her often, she rarely leaves this community
hundreds of kilometres from town
but sitting here on flour tins, not saying much
it feels like we're cousins who've grown old together

www.ingramcontent.com/pod-product-compliance
Lightning Source LLC
Chambersburg PA
CBHW062157100526
44589CB00014B/1861